Remembering the Dead

Around the World

Anita Ganeri

raintree

a Capstone company — publishers for children

Raintree is an imprint of Capstone Global Library Limited, a company incorporated in England and Wales having its registered office at 7 Pilgrim Street, London EC4V 6LB – Registered company number: 6695582

www.raintree.co.uk
myorders@raintree.co.uk

Edited by Clare Lewis and Brenda Haugen
Designed by Richard Parker
Picture research by Gina Kammer
Production by Helen McCreath
Originated by Capstone Global Library Ltd
Printed and bound in China by CTPS

ISBN 978 1 406 29897 0
19 18 17 16 15
10 9 8 7 6 5 4 3 2 1

British Library Cataloguing in Publication Data
A full catalogue record for this book is available from the British Library.

Acknowledgements
We would like to thank the following for permission to reproduce photographs:
Alamy: © Dinodia Photos, 23, © Guillermo Lopez Barrera, 7; AP Photo: Eternal Reefs Inc, 5; Capstone Press (map), throughout; Capstone Studio: Karon Dubke, 28, 29; Corbis: © David Bathgate, 17, © Gideon Mendel, 27, © Robert Wallis, 14, National Geographic Society/© Paul Chesley, 9; Getty Images: ADALBERTO ROQUE, 19, DOUG KANTER, 18, NICOLAS ASFOURI, 8, PHILIPPE LOPEZ, 12, Richard Ellis, 6; Glow Images: Robert Harding/Tim Graham, 22; iStockphoto: EyeJoy, 11, mariusss, 10; National Geographic Creative: IRA BLOCK, 13; Newscom: Eagle Visions P/Craig Lovell, 24, EPA/KIM LUDBROOK, 26, Godong/Philippe Lissac, 15, Mohamed Kadri Xinhua News Agency, 16, REUTERS/ LUC GNAGO, 20, ZUMA Press/Laura Embry, 21, ZUMAPRESS/Subhash Sharma, 25; Shutterstock: Brandon Bourdages, cover

We would like to thank Dr. Suzanne Owen for her invaluable help in the preparation of this book.

Every effort has been made to contact copyright holders of material reproduced in this book. Any omissions will be rectified in subsequent printings if notice is given to the publisher.

All the Internet addresses (URLs) given in this book were valid at the time of going to press. However, due to the dynamic nature of the Internet, some addresses may have changed, or sites may have changed or ceased to exist since publication. While the author and publisher regret any inconvenience this may cause readers, no responsibility for any such changes can be accepted by either the author or the publisher.

Contents

Remembering loved ones 4

Day of the Dead 6

Smoking ceremony 8

Jewish funeral 10

Funeral gifts 12

Mourning clothes around the world 14

Watched by angels 16

Jazz funeral 18

Coffins around the world 20

Many lives 22

Sky burials 24

Turning the bones 26

Decorate a Day of the Dead skull 28

Glossary 30

Find out more 31

Index 32

Some words are shown in bold, **like this**. You can find out what they mean by looking in the glossary.

Remembering loved ones

In cultures around the world, important events in people's lives are marked with special customs and ceremonies. They help people to celebrate occasions, such as the birth of a baby, a wedding or to remember a person who has died. They are also a way of guiding people from one stage of their lives to the next. This book looks at how people from different cultures and religions mark a person's death.

Around the world, people carry out special ceremonies and **rituals** when a person dies. These include **funerals** and burials, and ways of **mourning** and showing grief. In some cultures, people believe in an afterlife or in **reincarnation** (being born again in a different body). In others, death is truly believed to mark the end of life.

BURIAL AT SEA

A company in the United States offers people the chance to become a "reef ball" when they die. A person's remains are **cremated**, then mixed with concrete to form a ball. The ball is added to an artificial reef which provides a habitat for fish and other sea life.

What do you think of becoming a "reef ball" when you die?

Day of the Dead

On 2 November, people in Mexico remember people who have died. This is called the Day of the Dead. The celebration dates back hundreds of years to the time of the **Aztecs**.

People decorate graves with flowers for the Day of the Dead.

SUGAR SKULLS

For the Day of the Dead, stalls everywhere sell little skulls made from sugar. They are white and decorated in colourful icing, foil and glitter. People give the skulls as gifts. The name of the person receiving the skull is written on the skull in icing.

Stalls offer sugar skulls for people to give as gifts.

In the days leading up to the Day of the Dead, people visit the graves of their loved ones and decorate them with flowers. They take food and drink, in case their loved ones are hungry or thirsty. They also put out offerings of food on **altars** at home. They leave the windows open at night so that the spirits of their loved ones can come in to eat.

On the day itself, families spend the whole day by the graves, saying prayers for the dead. Some people take a picnic, and tell stories about their loved ones. These stories are often funny. The Day of the Dead is supposed to be a happy time.

Smoking ceremony

Aboriginal people have lived in Australia for thousands of years. When a loved one dies in Aboriginal society, a "smoking ceremony" is held near the dead person's house. People place bunches of green leaves on a small fire to make smoke. The smoke is wafted over the house and mourners. People believe that the smoke will drive away evil spirits. The smoke also cleanses the place and marks a new beginning.

This man is blowing on a bunch of smouldering leaves to make fire for a smoking ceremony.

Mourners paint their faces with red ochre and gather for a smoking ceremony.

After the ceremony, there is a great feast with singing and dancing. The mourners paint themselves with red ochre (clay), again to scare away evil. Traditionally, in northern parts of Australia, the dead person's body is placed on top of a wooden platform outside the village and covered in leaves. Then it is left to rot away.

CEREMONY FOR A BABY

Smoking ceremonies are also held at other important times, such as the birth of a baby. Aboriginal people believe that the smoke will help the baby to grow up to be strong and healthy. If a child falls ill, another smoking ceremony is held to help it get better.

Jewish funeral

A **Jewish funeral** takes place as soon as possible after a person has died. This is usually within 24 hours. According to tradition, most Jews are buried, although today some are **cremated** instead.

The rabbi leads the prayers at an Orthodox Jewish funeral.

The Yahrzeit candle is lit on the anniversary of the person's death.

The funeral service is very simple, with a plain **coffin** and no flowers. This shows that everyone, rich or poor, is equal before God. At the **cemetery**, a **rabbi** leads the prayers and reads from the **Torah**, the Jewish holy book. He also talks about the life and achievements of the person who has died.

LIGHTING A CANDLE

Each year, on the anniversary of his or her death, the dead person's name is read out in the **synagogue**. At home, relatives light a special candle, called a Yahrzeit (say "yart-site") which burns for 24 hours. They also recite the Kaddish, which is the Jewish prayer for the dead.

For seven days after a death, the family stay at home to mourn their loved one. This is called "sitting Shivah" (*Shivah* means "seven"). Every evening, friends and relatives visit the house to offer prayers and sympathy to the family.

Funeral gifts

There are many rules around death in Chinese culture. People believe that bad luck will come to the family if it does not follow the rules properly.

At a **funeral** in China, family and friends bring **wreaths** of white flowers, such as irises. White is the traditional colour of **mourning** in Chinese culture. The flowers are placed around the body, which is laid in an open **coffin**. People also bring white envelopes, filled with money. This is given to the family to help pay for the funeral.

Flower stalls in China sell ready-made wreaths for funerals.

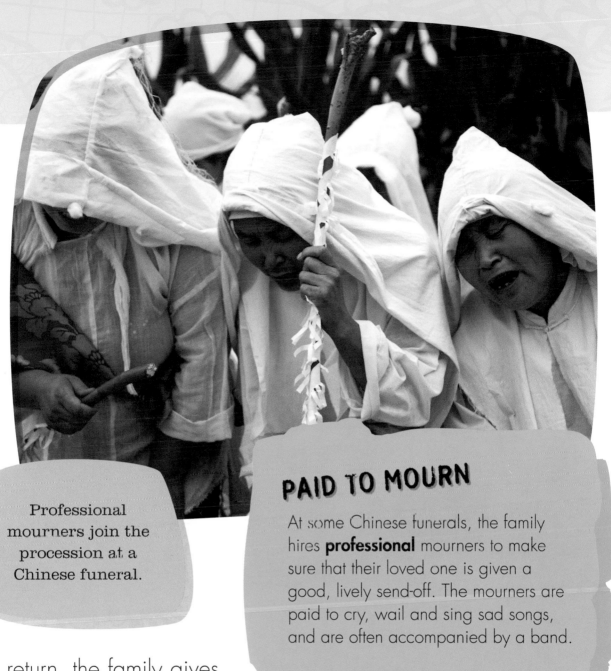

Professional mourners join the procession at a Chinese funeral.

PAID TO MOURN

At some Chinese funerals, the family hires **professional** mourners to make sure that their loved one is given a good, lively send-off. The mourners are paid to cry, wail and sing sad songs, and are often accompanied by a band.

In return, the family gives each guest a white or red envelope with a coin, a sweet, a handkerchief and a piece of red thread inside. The coin is to make sure that the guest returns home safely. Guests take the red thread home and tie it to the front door of their house to keep evil spirits away.

Mourning Clothes

Around the World

Colours of mourning

In different cultures, different colours are linked to death. In some countries, people wear black clothes to **funerals**. The black colour matches the sadness of the occasion. In Europe, this tradition dates back to Roman times when men wore dark-coloured **togas** during times of **mourning**. In some countries, such as Spain, **widows** may wear black clothes for the rest of their lives.

Japanese mourners traditionally wear black.

Chinese colours

In Chinese culture, only the dead person's closest relatives wear black. Any grandchildren, aunts, uncles and cousins wear blue. Other mourners, who are not as close to the dead person, wear white and other bright colours. People do not wear red clothes because red is the colour of happiness.

Widows in white

In the **Hindu** religion, white is the colour of mourning. A Hindu widow wears a plain white **sari**, with very little jewellery. She also removes the red mark that she has worn on her forehead since she was married.

From the time of her husband's death, a Hindu widow dresses in white.

Mourning rings

For hundreds of years in the United Kingdom, it was the custom for people to wear mourning rings to remember loved ones who had died. The rings were often made from gold and black **jet** and, often, a lock of the dead person's hair.

Watched by angels

If possible, a **Muslim funeral** should take place on the same day that a person dies. The body is washed and wrapped in white cloth. It is taken in a **coffin** to the **mosque**, where the **imam** recites the funeral prayers. After this, the coffin is taken to the **cemetery**.

Muslims are buried facing towards the holy city of Mecca. During their lives, this is the direction they face when they pray every day. The grave is marked with a simple stone.

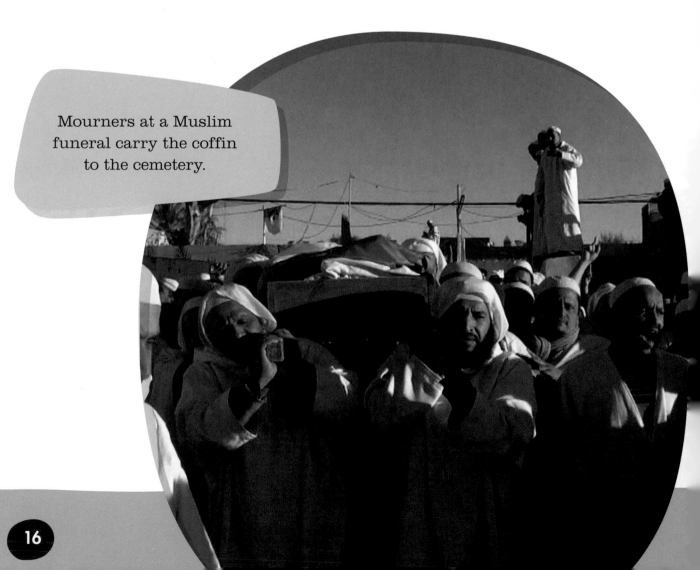

Mourners at a Muslim funeral carry the coffin to the cemetery.

Muslims are sad to lose a loved one but are comforted in their faith. They believe that every person is watched by two angels, who keep a record of the person's good and bad deeds. This record is handed to **Allah** on the Day of Judgement. People who have lived good lives, according to Allah's wishes, will go to Paradise. Wicked people will go to Hell.

DYING WORDS

The **Prophet Muhammad** said that the last words a dying Muslim should hear are those of the Shahadah. This is a special prayer which expresses what Muslims believe.

"There is no God but Allah.

And Muhammad is his messenger."

In a Muslim cemetery, the gravestones face towards the holy city of Mecca.

Jazz funeral

In the city of New Orleans, USA, some people from African-American communities, mostly musicians, have a **jazz funeral**. A funeral begins with a service in a Christian church. Then a jazz band plays sad, marching music as the **coffin** is taken to the **cemetery**. After leaving the cemetery, the music changes and the band strikes up much livelier, happier tunes. Everyone sings and dances along to celebrate the life of the person who has died.

This jazz band is playing at a jazz funeral in New Orleans.

The roots of the jazz funeral date back to Africa. Music is an important part of funerals in many African countries. The Yoruba people of Nigeria dance, sing and play drums. They believe that this helps to keep the dead person's spirit happy. The **ancestors** of many African-Americans came to the United States as slaves and brought their customs with them.

FUNERAL MUSIC

Around the world, music is often played at funerals. This may be a religious song, such as a hymn, or a piece of music that had a special connection to the dead person. In one poll of the most popular funeral songs, "My Way" by Frank Sinatra topped the list.

A Yoruba funeral is marked with dancing, singing and drumming.

Coffins Around the World

After a person dies, his or her body may be placed in a **coffin**, ready to be buried or **cremated**. Coffins come in many sizes and shapes.

This fish-shaped coffin in Ghana is designed for a fisherman.

Amazing coffins

In Ghana, some people are buried in brightly coloured coffins that represent their life or work. Examples include fish- or boat-shaped coffins for fishermen; Bible-shaped coffins for church-goers; piano-shaped coffins for musicians; and even camera-shaped coffins for photographers.

Eco-coffins

In some Western countries, people choose to be buried or cremated in coffins that do not harm the environment. This means using coffins made from materials that rot away quickly and easily, such as bamboo, willow, and even cloth and cardboard.

Another unusual eco-coffin is shaped like an egg and made from **bioplastic**. The body is placed inside and the egg is planted in the ground, like a bulb. A tree is planted on top.

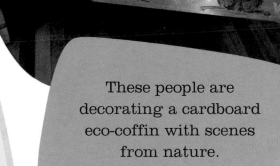

These people are decorating a cardboard eco-coffin with scenes from nature.

Tree burials

The Caviteno people of the Philippines do not use coffins for their dead. Instead, they bury them standing upright inside a hollowed-out tree trunk. The dying person chooses the tree when he or she falls ill or grows very old.

Many lives

Hindus do not believe that death is the end of life. They believe in **reincarnation**, where a person's soul lives on after death and is born again in a new body – human or animal. A person's next life depends on how they lived their current life. If they have acted well, they will be reborn in a better life. If they have acted badly, their next life will be a worse one.

At a Hindu funeral, the body is burnt on a funeral pyre.

This Indian man is scattering the ashes of his father in the River Ganges.

Funeral pyre

At a Hindu **funeral**, the body is always **cremated**. Traditionally in India, the body is placed on a large platform of logs and sandalwood, called a **pyre**. The eldest son, or a close male relative, walks about the pyre seven times. Then he lights the fire while a priest chants verses from the Hindu sacred books.

SACRED RIVER

Three days after the funeral, the relatives collect the ashes. If possible, they scatter them in the River Ganges. It is a sacred river for Hindus. They believe that the water of the Ganges washes away people's sins.

After the funeral, there are 10 or 12 days of **mourning**. On the last day, Hindus believe that the person's soul has found a new body.

Sky burials

In much of Tibet, the ground is too rocky or hard to dig a grave and there is not much firewood for building **funeral pyres**. A dead body is carried to a mountainside and left for the vultures to eat. Most Tibetans are **Buddhists**. They believe that this is a good and generous way of disposing of a body because it provides food for other living things.

BIRDS AND ANGELS

Like **Hindus**, Buddhists believe that a dead person's soul is born again in a new body. Tibetans believe that the vultures are like angels. They carry the dead person's soul up into the heavens where it waits to be reborn.

These vultures gather round a sky burial site in Tibet.

Towers of silence

According to **Zoroastrian** beliefs, a dead body is unclean. It must not be allowed to touch earth, fire or water. To avoid this, a dead person's body is placed on top of a tall stone tower for the vultures to eat. The tower is called a dakhma, or tower of silence. Some time later, the bones are collected in a pit in the centre of the tower. Over a long time, they gradually wear away.

Zoroastrians place dead bodies in towers of silence, like this one in India.

Turning the bones

The people of Madagascar have an unusual ceremony for remembering their dead. It is called famadihana which means "the turning of the bones". Every five or seven years, a family visits their family tomb where the bones of their dead relatives lie, wrapped in cloths. The bones are taken out and sprayed with perfume. Then, as a band plays, members of the family take turns in dancing with the bones.

People carry the wrapped bones of their ancestors at famadihana.

Families dance together as they carry the bones in white cloths.

This ceremony may sound gruesome but in Malagasy culture, it is a way of thanking and showing respect to those who have died. People tell stories about their relatives and ask for their blessing. It is also a chance for a family reunion – relatives come from across the country to take part in the celebrations.

RESPECT FOR ANCESTORS

In Malagasy culture, people show great respect to their razana (**ancestors**). They believe that the ancestors have the power to affect the lives and fortunes of the living, and that there will be great hardship or trouble if they are offended.

Afterwards, the bones are wrapped in fresh cloths and placed back in the tomb.

Decorate a Day of the Dead skull

YOU WILL NEED

- Two sheets of scrap paper
- Large bowl
- Flour
- Water
- PVA glue
- Strainer
- Baking paper
- Paints and other decorations
- Scissors
- Paintbrush

Mexicans celebrate the Day of the Dead by making beautiful sugar skulls (see page 7). They are decorated to look friendly and colourful, and given as gifts. Make your own skull decorations using scrap paper.

1 Tear the paper into small squares, and put them into a bowl. Add a tablespoon of flour.

2 Ask an adult to help you add hot water from the hot tap. Leave the paper and flour to soak for three hours.

3 Rub and squish the paper with your fingers to make a pulp. Tip the mixture into a strainer, and squeeze out as much water as possible.

4 Put the pulp back into the bowl. Add a tablespoon of PVA glue, and knead with your hands until the mixture feels like clay.

5 Trace the outline of a skull on a piece of baking paper. Build up skull shape using small balls of the paper pulp.

6 Use the bottom of a pencil to make dents for eyes, and the pointed tip of the pencil to mark the nose and teeth.

7 Leave the paper skull to dry for two to three days. Then add a coat of white paint.

9 Trim away the paper at the edges. Brush on a coat of watered-down PVA glue to seal your design.

8 Decorate your skull using bright colours and shapes such as flowers, dots and swirls. Mexicans often add beads, sequins and glitter, too.

Remember, these skulls are just for decoration and NOT for eating!

Glossary

Allah Islamic name for God, in the Arabic language

altar place where offerings such as food and flowers are made to gods and ancestors

ancestor relative from the past

Aztecs people who lived in Mexico hundreds of years ago

bioplastic type of plastic made from plant oil that breaks down more quickly than ordinary plastic

Buddhist person who follows the religion of Buddhism

cemetery place where dead people are buried

coffin box in which a dead person's body is buried or cremated

cremated when a dead person's body is burned

funeral ceremony at which a dead person's body is buried or cremated

Hindu person who follows the Hindu religion

imam religious leader

jazz lively type of music

jet hard, black stone

Jewish connected with the religion of Judaism. A Jew is a person who follows Judaism.

mosque place of worship

mourning feeling and showing sadness that a person has died

Muslim person who follows the religion of Islam

professional person who is paid for what they do as a job

Prophet Muhammad last and greatest in a line of messengers sent by Allah to teach people how to live in the Muslim religion

pyre pile of wood on which a dead body is placed for cremation

rabbi Jewish religious teacher

reincarnation belief that a person is born again when he or she dies

ritual ceremony with set ways of doing things

sari traditional dress worn by many women in India

synagogue Jewish place of worship

toga robe worn by some men in Roman times

Torah part of the Jewish holy book

widow wife whose husband has died

wreath ring of flowers, sometimes placed on a person's grave

Zoroastrian person who follows the religion of Zoroastrianism

Find out more

Books

Around the World in 500 Festivals, Steve Davey (Kuperard, 2013)

Encyclopedia of World Religions (Internet-linked Encyclopedias),
    Susan Meredith (Usborne, 2010)

What Do You Believe? Aled Jones (Dorling Kindersley, 2011)

Websites

www.bbc.co.uk/nature/humanplanetexplorer

This brilliant website has stunning photos and video clips showing how people live around the world. There is a section on life events, including birth, childhood, coming of age, finding a partner and death.

www.bbc.co.uk/religion/religions

Find out more about the world's religions on this fact-packed website. There is also an interfaith calendar which looks at celebrations and holy days in different cultures.

Further research

It is sad when someone dies but it is also a time for remembering the happy times that you shared with that person. Some people write poems or stories to help them remember loved ones. Can you find some of these in books or on the internet?

Index

Aboriginal people 8–9
African-Americans 18–19
angels 17, 24
ashes, scattering 23
Australia 8–9

bad luck 12
black clothes 14, 15
Buddhists 24

candles 11
cemeteries 11, 16,
    17, 18
China 12–13, 14, 15
clothes and colours
    14–15
coffins 11, 12, 16,
    18, 20–21
cremation 4, 10, 21, 23

dancing 9, 18, 19, 26
Day of Judgement 17
Day of the Dead 6–7, 28

eco-coffins 21
England 15
evil spirits 8, 9, 13

famadihana 26–27
flowers 6, 7, 12
food and feasts 7, 9
funerals 4, 10–11,
    12–13, 14, 16,
    18–19, 22–23

Ghana 20
gifts 7, 12, 13

Hell 17
Hindus 15, 22–23

imams 16
India 25

jazz funerals 18–19
Jewish funerals 10–11

Kaddish 11

Madagascar 26–27
Mecca 16, 17
Mexico 6–7, 28
mosques 16
Muhammad, Prophet 17
music 18–19
Muslims 16–17

Nigeria 19

Paradise 17
Philippines 21
prayers 7, 11, 16, 17
professional mourners
    13, 14
pyres 22, 23

rabbis 10, 11
"reef balls" 4, 5
reincarnation 4, 22,
    23, 24
rings, mourning 15

Shahadah 17
sitting Shivah 11
skulls 7, 28–29
sky burials 9, 24–25
smoking ceremony 8–9
Spain 14
synagogues 11

Tibet 24
Torah 11
towers of silence 25
turning of the bones
    ceremony 26–27

United States 18–19

Yahrzeit candles 11
Yoruba people 19

Zoroastrians 25